EDGE BOOKS

FULL THROTTLE

SPORT BIKES

by
Hans Hetrick

Consultant:
Dan Smith
Former Resource Development Director
The AMA's Motorcycle Hall of Fame Museum
Pickerington, Ohio

CAPSTONE PRESS
a capstone imprint

Edge Books are published by Capstone Press,
151 Good Counsel Drive, P.O. Box 669, Mankato, Minnesota 56002.
www.capstonepub.com

Books published by Capstone Press are manufactured with paper containing at least 10 percent post-consumer waste.

Library of Congress Cataloging-in-Publication Data
Hetrick, Hans, 1973–
Sport bikes / by Hans Hetrick.
p. cm.—(Edge books. full throttle)
Includes bibliographical references and index.
Summary: "Describes sport bikes, including their history, design, and the road course races they participate in, such as MotoGP and the Superbike World Championship"—Provided by publisher.
ISBN 978-1-4296-4751-9 (library binding)
1. Motorcycles—Juvenile literature. 2. Motorcycles, Racing—Juvenile literature. I. Title. II. Series.
TL440.15.H48 2011
796.7'5—dc22 2010000066

Editorial Credits
Carrie Braulick Sheely, editor; Matt Bruning, designer; Laura Manthe, production specialist

Photo Credits
Alamy: Bernie Epstein, 10, imagebroker, 18, Joe Fox Motorsport, 15, Oleksiy Maksymenko Photography, 7, Optikat, 14, TavlikosPhoto MotorSports, 17; Brian Nelson, 4; Capstone Studio/Karon Dubke, 7; Courtesy of American Honda Motor Co., Inc., 7, 19; Dreamstime: Totalphoto, cover; Getty Images Inc.: AFP, 12, AFP/Andrew Yates, 24, AFP/Javier Soriano, 27, Barry Harcourt, 6, Ian Walton, 29, Keystone/Terry Fincher, 9, Quinn Rooney, 28; Shutterstock: afaizal, 16, 20, 21, 23; SSPL via Getty Images, 8

Artistic Effects
Dreamstime: In-finity, Michaelkovachev; iStockphoto: Michael Irwin, Russell Tate; Shutterstock: Els Jooren, Fedorov Oleksiy, javarman, jgl247, Marilyn Volan, Pocike

Printed in the United States of America in Stevens Point, Wisconsin.
012011
006049R

Table of Contents

1 THE CHASE IS ON!

Ben Spies was playing catch-up on his Suzuki GSX-R1000. Spies knew he didn't have much time. Only a few laps remained in the 2008 American Motorcyclist Association (AMA) Superbike race at California's Auto Club Speedway.

At the start of the race, Mat Mladin had jumped into the lead. By the 24th lap, Mladin's lead over Spies had grown to more than three seconds. That's when Spies started chipping away at the gap.

Ben Spies (#1) trailed behind Mat Mladin (#6) for much of the 2008 Auto Club Speedway race.

By the 28th and final lap, Spies was right on Mladin's rear tire. Out of the final turn, Spies got into Mladin's **draft** in the straightaway. Just before the finish line, Spies shot past Mladin. He won the race by only 0.011 second. It was the closest finish in the racetrack's history.

"That was a tough race," said Spies. " ... The last 10 laps I was just out of control. I couldn't believe how fast we were riding out there ... Every time I could get it wide open, I would. I was just trying to go as fast as I can."

The 2008 Auto Club Speedway race was wild. Yet it's only one of many great road races sport bike fans have seen. Packed with thrills and spills, each one promises heart-pounding excitement.

draft—a pocket of air that lies behind a moving vehicle; moving into the draft of a leading racer helps a trailing racer go faster

BUILT TO PERFORM

A sport bike is a high-performance motorcycle built for paved roads. Sport bikes have powerful engines and strong, lightweight frames. One of the fastest **factory** models is the Suzuki GSX-R1000. It blasts from 0 to 60 miles (96 kilometers) per hour in less than three seconds. Its top speed is around 186 miles (300 km) per hour. Sport bikes used for racing go even faster.

The GSX-R1000's first-class performance has earned it many race wins.

factory—describes a vehicle with few or no changes to its original factory-installed parts

Which Motorcycle is Which?

Cruisers

Like sport bikes, cruisers are street bikes, which means they're made for riding on streets and other paved public roads. But cruisers are bulkier and heavier than sport bikes. They are made for longer, easier rides. Riders sit up straight with their feet forward. The handlebars are usually set near the rider's chest. Harley-Davidson makes some of the most popular cruisers.

Off-road Motorcycles

Off-road motorcycles are called dirt bikes. They are made to ride easily over gravel, mud, and other loose surfaces. Dirt bike frames sit up high off the ground. The motorcycles have large knobs on their tires for good grip.

Dual-sport Motorcycles

A dual-sport motorcycle is a combination of a street bike and a dirt bike. Turn signals, headlights, and mirrors make them legal to ride on the streets. Like off-road motorcycles, their frames sit high off the ground.

2 Sport Bike History

In 1885, Gottlieb Daimler invented one of the first useful gasoline engines. He put it on a two-wheeled vehicle, making the first gasoline-powered motorcycle. Daimler's motorcycle was basically a bicycle with a giant engine between the wheels.

As motorcycle companies sprang up in the early 1900s, so did motorcycle races. Sport bikes have their roots in Europe's MotoGP road races. At first, these popular races were held on public roads that were closed off for the events. Eventually, the races were moved to paved racetracks.

Gottlieb Daimler's wooden motorcycle had two small wheels at the back for balance.

MV Agusta rider John Surtees racked up four MotoGP World Championship titles from 1956 to 1960.

In 1949, the first MotoGP World Championship was held. At the time, Italian companies MV Agusta and Moto Guzzi made the top race bikes. In England, BSA, Norton, and Triumph were successful manufacturers. But Japanese companies Honda, Suzuki, Kawasaki, and Yamaha also wanted to make their mark on MotoGP. In the 1960s, they began winning championships in the 125-cc and 250-cc classes.

THE CAFÉ RACERS

While manufacturers battled in MotoGP, café racers set the stage for high-performance bikes to reach the public. Café racers were young British motorcyclists with a taste for adventure. They especially liked testing the limits of their bikes.

To reach higher speeds, café racers began changing, or modifying, their motorcycles. The café racers wanted their factory bikes to look and perform like the British MotoGP bikes. They added lightweight gas tanks, low clip-on handlebars, and rear-set foot pegs to their bikes. Then they cruised the streets on their souped-up machines.

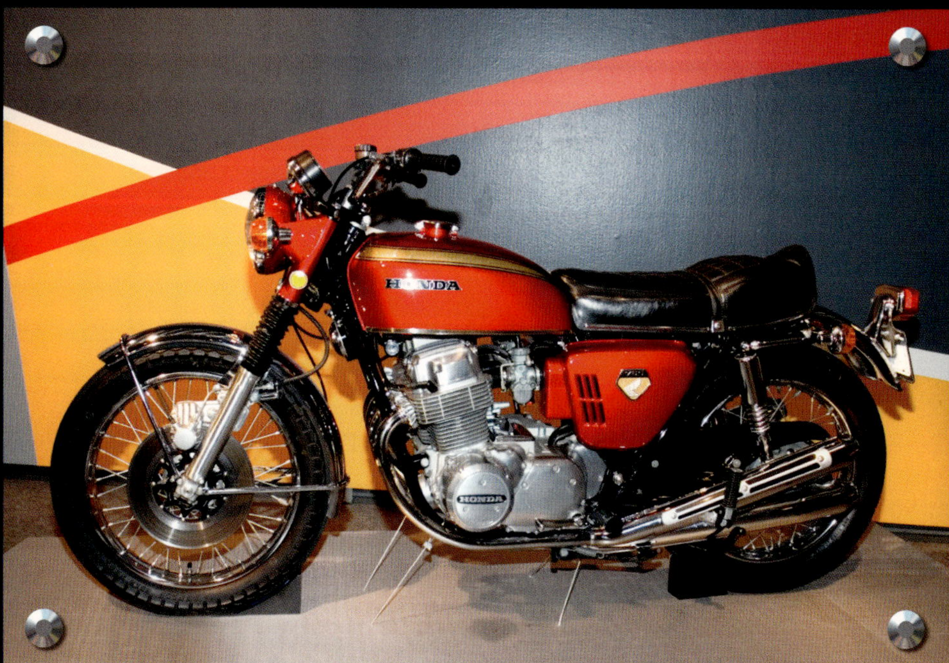

The 1969 Honda CB750 in the famous candy apple red color continues to be a popular collectors' bike.

Power to the Masses

Manufacturers soon realized that fast bikes didn't have to be just for the racetracks. Popular early sport bike models sold to the public included the Triumph Trident and the BSA Rocket 3.

In 1969, Honda stomped on the competition with the CB750. The CB750 was the first mass-produced motorcycle with a four-**cylinder** engine. Motorcycles before it had only two or three cylinders. This powerful engine pushed the bike to a top speed of 125 miles (201 km) per hour. The bike also came with strong front disc brakes and an electric start.

cylinder—a hollow area inside an engine in which fuel burns to create power

Fast Fact: *Café racers often modified the Triumph Bonneville and the Norton Dominator.*

THE RISE OF THE BIG FOUR

The CB750 was just the first of many Japanese motorcycles to shock the world. Suzuki, Kawasaki, and Yamaha joined Honda in turning out the world's most advanced bikes. These manufacturers became known as the big four.

Throughout the 1970s, the Japanese companies experimented with different types of engines and frame designs. Their ideas soon came together in a rock-solid package. This design became known as the Universal Japanese Motorcycle, or UJM.

Fairings on Japanese motorcycles of the late 1970s helped the bikes slice through the air.

UJMs had an advanced design. They featured powerful four-cylinder engines. They had steel-tube frames, aluminum wheels, and strong front and rear **suspension systems**. These features reduced the motorcycles' weight. At the same time, they gave riders excellent handling. Plastic frame coverings, or fairings, reduced wind resistance. The Kawasaki GPZ900R Ninja and the Suzuki GSX-R750 reached top speeds near 160 miles (257 km) per hour.

suspension system—a system of springs and shock absorbers designed to reduce a bike's up-and-down movements and keep the bike stable during braking and cornering

Fast Fact: *Early high-performance bikes were known as superbikes. Today the word "superbike" usually refers only to the most powerful sport bikes.*

Sport Bikes Around the World

Over time, sport bikes gained more fans in the United States. In 1976, the American Motorcyclist Association (AMA) created the Superbike Championship road-racing series. The series featured sport bikes that had been slightly modified from their factory versions.

Fast Fact: *U.S. manufacturer Buell produced sport bikes from 1983 to 2009. In 2009, the company won its first pro AMA road-racing championship.*

The Honda CBR900RR handled especially well around corners.

In the late 1980s and early 1990s, sport bike engines became even more powerful. To help the bikes handle all the power, many companies switched from steel frames to aluminum frames. Using aluminum reduced weight but maintained strength. Manufacturers also improved braking systems. Once again, Honda left competitors in the dust with the 1992 CBR900RR Fireblade. The bike's light weight and **compact** design gave riders excellent handling.

Today, Japan's big four are still going strong. But they aren't alone. Companies worldwide, such as BMW of Germany and Ducati of Italy, all build competitive sport bikes.

compact—describes a close-fitting design that saves space

3 TECHNOLOGY MEETS TWO WHEELS

Today's sport bikes perform at a mind-boggling level. Manufacturers are always in search of the perfect balance of power and control. They consider every detail—even the tiniest screw on the rearview mirrors. Their hard work brings countless moments of fun to everyday sport bike owners. It also puts the best bikes on the racetracks. Bikes that win races create a higher demand for their street-going versions. This idea is captured in the famous phrase "Win on Sunday, sell on Monday."

The popularity of road racing around the world helps build demand for street-going sport bikes.

FRONT FORK SETUP

Sport bikes have a different front fork setup than most other motorcycles. Think of a chopper. Many choppers have a long wheelbase, or distance between the front and rear wheels. The front wheel sticks out far ahead of the handlebars. The long angle, or rake, of the front forks makes the chopper more stable while traveling in a straight line. But it also makes the chopper more difficult to turn. Sport bikes are the complete opposite. Their short wheelbase and short-angled rake allow them to turn quickly and smoothly.

A sport bike's front wheel sits close to the frame. This design helps the bike take corners at high speeds.

ENGINES

Sport bike engines come in many types. The most common design is the inline four-cylinder. Two-cylinder and three-cylinder inline engines are also used. Cylinders in an inline engine are set in a straight line. In other sport bike engines, the cylinders are set in a "V" shape. For example, a two-cylinder engine in a "V" shape is called a V-twin.

Engine size is measured in cubic centimeters, or cc. Sport bike engine size ranges from about 250 cc to about 1,350 cc. Sport bikes with engine sizes over 1,000 cc are sometimes called superbikes. Superbikes represent the top level in most road-racing series.

Ducati's trellis frame is welded in a triangular pattern for extra strength.

The two wide beams of the twin-spar frame are sometimes left uncovered by the fairings.

FRAMES

Most sport bike frames are made of aluminum. This metal is lightweight yet very strong. The twin-spar frame is the most common design. It has two strong beams that wrap around the engine and join together.

Trellis frames are common on Italian sport bikes like Ducatis and MV Agustas. These frames wrap around the engine using several metal tubes.

Suspension Systems

Strong suspension systems make quick stops and high-speed cornering possible. For front suspension, almost every sport bike uses telescopic front forks. Each fork includes one big shock absorber with a spring on the inside. Most sport bikes have upside-down forks. With this design, the heavier fork parts are at the top. Moving the weight higher up improves handling. Cartridges in the forks allow riders to adjust the suspension.

In upside-down telescopic front forks, the larger outer tubes are at the top. The smaller inner tubes are at the bottom. The inner tubes slide inside the outer tubes to absorb force.

The most common type of rear suspension is the swing arm. A swing arm connects to the frame and holds the rear wheel. One or two large shock absorbers are installed between the swing arm and the frame. Swing arms provide the best shock absorption of any rear suspension.

Many MotoGP bikes have swing arms made of carbon fiber to reduce weight.

BRAKES

Nearly every sport bike today uses disc brakes—two on the front and one on the rear. The brakes usually have multi-piston calipers. This design improves control by making sure the pads push evenly against the discs.

TIRES

Sport bike tires are made with soft rubber. They're also strong and wide. All of these features help them stick to the road and make high-speed cornering possible.

In dry weather, race bikes use tires with a smooth surface. Called slicks, they provide better grip than tires with a lot of tread. The tires are heated before races so that riders can begin racing with as much grip as possible.

FAIRINGS

Sport bike fairings are designed to reduce wind resistance. They are made of lightweight materials such as plastic or carbon fiber. Full fairings are best at reducing wind resistance. They cover the engine, the frame, and the front of the bike. Half-fairing bikes have a windshield and a small front shell. A bike with no fairings is called a naked bike.

Sport Bikes at a Glance

Weight:	280 to 500 pounds (127 to 227 kilograms)
Fairings:	usually full; made of plastic or carbon fiber
Top speed:	about 120 to 185 miles (193 to 298 kilometers) per hour for factory bikes; more than 200 miles (322 kilometers) per hour for race bikes
Engine size:	about 250 to 1,350 cc
Engine type:	inline or V
Frame:	twin-spar aluminum, aluminum-tube trellis, and steel-tube trellis
Frame material:	usually aluminum; some race bikes use carbon fiber
Horsepower:	up to 190
Transmission:	manual with six gears

The Yamaha YZR-M1 of MotoGP racer Valentino Rossi sits with its tire warmers on before a race.

4 ON THE RACETRACK

Sport bikes are built for speed. But riders can't unleash the full power of their bikes on public roads. That's why many organizations set up official races. Like in the past, road races are the most popular races for sport bikes. Some motorcycle clubs set up road races at local tracks. The AMA Pro American Superbike, the Superbike World Championship, and MotoGP are the most famous professional racing series.

American Ben Spies leads a Superbike World Championship race in 2009.

ROAD RACING BASICS

Races in professional series are held at a number of different courses during the spring and summer. The courses are chock-full of challenges, including **chicanes** and tight turns called hairpins. Pit stops are rare, and most races last about 45 minutes.

Racers earn starting positions based on qualifying times. Points are awarded based on where riders place in the race. The first-place finisher receives the most points. The points given decrease the lower a racer finishes. At the end of the series, the racer with the most points wins the championship.

The MotoGP and the Superbike World Championship series also award a championship title to a manufacturer. During the series, manufacturers earn points for wins just like the riders do.

chicane—a series of tight turns in opposite directions

AMA Pro American Superbike

The AMA Pro American Superbike series runs races at about 10 U.S. tracks. It features the most powerful factory motorcycles available, such as the Ducati 1098R and the Yamaha R1. Rules allow race teams to make changes to a few parts, such as the brakes and fuel tanks. The series has made racers such as Ben Spies, Mat Mladin, and Ben and Eric Bostrom into road-racing superstars.

Superbike World Championship

The Superbike World Championship series got its start in 1988. It is the newest pro road-racing series. Like in the AMA Superbike series, World Superbike racers ride tuned-up factory models. The bikes have engine sizes in the 1,000-cc range. The races are run at tracks throughout the world. Popular riders of recent years include American Ben Spies, Japan's Noriyuki Haga, and Italy's Michel Fabrizio.

MOTOGP

Like the Superbike World Championship series, MotoGP features riders from around the world. But MotoGP bikes are very different from bikes in other pro road-racing series. Factory models are not available for the public to buy. Instead, race teams specially build their bikes for the series. Race teams must follow rules for engine size, weight, and other features. The season includes 18 races that are held in different countries around the world.

Fast Fact: Italian MotoGP rider Valentino Rossi is sometimes called the GOAT, or Greatest Of All Time. Rossi has won nine MotoGP World Championships. He is also first in all-time race wins.

MORE THRILLS TO COME

Ben Spies chases down race leader Noriyuki Haga at a 2009 Superbike World Championship race in Australia.

Ben Spies moved to the Superbike World Championship series from the AMA Superbike series for the 2009 season. There he found a new rival to replace Mat Mladin—Noriyuki Haga. In the end, Spies won the championship by just eight points.

The first-place duel between Haga and Spies was one of the most exciting in the series' history. Battles like it are part of what makes road racing so popular. No one knows what the future holds for sport bikes. But one thing seems certain. As road racers demand more of their machines, sport bike design can only get better.

Isle of Man TT

The Isle of Man is a small island in the Irish Sea between England and Ireland. Every year in May and June, the island closes off its public roads and holds motorcycle races. The first motorcycle race was held in 1905. From 1949 to 1976, the Isle of Man TT was part of the MotoGP series. Today the Isle of Man TT races are no longer part of a series. But they are still very popular. Thousands of fans flock to the island each year to watch some of the world's best road racers compete.

GLOSSARY

chicane (shi-KAYN)—a series of tight turns going in opposite directions on a race course

compact (kahm-PAKT)—put together closely in a way that saves space

cylinder (SI-luhn-duhr)—a hollow area inside an engine in which fuel burns to produce power

draft (DRAFT)—a pocket of air that lies behind a moving vehicle; moving into the draft of a leading racer helps a trailing racer go faster

factory (FAK-tuh-ree)—describes a vehicle that has all or most of the parts that were installed at the factory

fairings (FAYR-ings)—the plastic coverings that surround most sport bikes; fairings are shaped to reduce wind resistance

suspension system (suh-SPEN-shuhn SISS-tuhm)—a system of springs and shock absorbers that smooth out bumps and provide stability

tread (TRED)—a series of bumps and deep grooves on a tire

READ MORE

Gifford, Clive. *Extreme Motorcycle Racing.* Extreme Adventures! Mankato, Minn.: Capstone Press, 2010.

Graham, Ian. *Superbikes.* Designed for Success. Chicago: Heinemann Library, 2008.

Young, Jeff C. *Motorcycles: The Ins and Outs of Superbikes, Choppers, and Other Motorcycles.* RPM. Mankato, Minn.: Capstone Press, 2010.

INTERNET SITES

FactHound offers a safe, fun way to find Internet sites related to this book. All of the sites on FactHound have been researched by our staff.

Here's all you do:

Visit *www.facthound.com*

FactHound will fetch the best sites for you!

Index